Catherine Oakes -

Advent - 1958

CHRISTMAS
AND
ITS CUSTOMS

CHRISTMAS

AND

ITS CUSTOMS

A Brief Study by
CHRISTINA HOLE

Illustrated by
T. EVERY-CLAYTON

M. BARROWS AND COMPANY, INC.
New York   *1958*

Contents

1 THE BEGINNINGS OF CHRISTMAS . . 7

2 THE CHRISTMAS SEASON 14

3 GARLANDS AND GREENERY . . . 21

4 FIRE AND LIGHT 29

5 GIFTS AND GREETINGS 35

6 THE GIFT-BRINGER 42

7 THE CHRISTMAS FEAST 51

8 CAROLS 58

9 THE NEW YEAR 65

10 TWELFTH-NIGHT AND CHRISTMAS-
   END 72

11 CHRISTMAS LEGENDS AND
   SUPERSTITIONS 83

   BOOKS ABOUT CHRISTMAS . . . 92

   INDEX 93

1

The Beginnings of Christmas

CHRISTMAS began nearly two thousand years ago when Christ was born in a stable in a small Jewish town. Few people knew about it at the time, and, of those who did, only a handful dimly realized that something stupendous had occurred. Yet what happened then changed the whole history of the world, and it is that event, and that only, which gives a meaning to Christmas now. It is true that there were joyful celebrations at the Winter Solstice long before the Christian Era, but these were pagan festivals which faded with the beliefs from which they sprang; and if Christmas was nothing more to us than a holiday among other holidays, it would long since have degenerated into a mere orgy of eating and drinking, and might by now have disappeared altogether.

Fortunately for us all, that has not happened. Christmas still remains the Feast of the Nativity, the first of that great cycle of feasts and fasts by which the Church remembers the splendid events of the Christian religion, and the most intimate of them all, because, being the birthday of the Christ Child, it is the supreme festival of children and of every human family. Spiritually and materially, it is a day of new beginnings, of light and warmth and the revival of hope. In the Northern Hemisphere, where it was first observed, its midwinter date gives it a special character, so that its very name conjures up a picture of frost and snow and evergreens, of fires and candlelight indoors, and of the first, almost imperceptible, lengthening of daylight hours outside. It is the one season of the year when homely kindliness, generosity and gaiety triumph, if only briefly, over drab materialism and selfishness, and the angel's message of goodwill sounds again even for those who do not believe in angels. In fact, as has been truly said, Christmas is not only a date in time and a recurring festival; it is also an experience of the human heart, centuries old by now and vividly colored by ancient thought and custom, yet as new and fresh every year as the universal hope it represents.

It was not observed as a separate feast until the

fourth century A.D. Before that time the Nativity and the Epiphany were celebrated together on January 6. When the new festival was instituted, the date had to be chosen arbitrarily, because no one knew for certain (nor does any one know now) on what day Christ was born. A very early Christian tradition, recorded by St. Chrysostom and other writers, said it was on December 25, but this was no more than a tradition, and many learned men disputed it. Yet even an uncertain legend has its value when exact knowledge is lacking, and after a very careful inquiry into the available evidence, Pope Julius I (A.D. 337–352) decided that the traditional date was probably the true one.

There was also another consideration which almost certainly influenced the choice of December 25 as the Feast of the Nativity. It was the policy of the early Church to transform pagan festivals wherever possible instead of trying to abolish them, and by giving ancient practices a Christian significance, to purify and preserve for the new faith whatever was innocent and deeply loved in the old. In the yet unconverted world of the fourth century, December 25 was already a sacred day for thousands of people throughout the Roman Empire. It was *Dies Natalis Invicti Solis,* the Birthday of the Unconquered Sun. It was the chief festival of the Phrygian god, Attis, and also of Mithras, whose cult was carried to Britain and other lands by the Roman army. It fell between the week-long feast of the Saturnalia, which began on December 17, and the Kalends of January, which ushered in the new year; and it coincided more or less closely with all those midwinter festivals at which the primitive peoples of Europe and Asia had celebrated, from time immemorial, the sun's rebirth at the Winter Solstice. The Church, by making it also the Feast of the Nativity, sanctified and renewed it, and thus as Christianity gained ground, slowly but surely changed its ancient worship of the material sun into that of the true Light of the World.

Many of our Christmas customs have their roots in pagan ceremonies that were already hoary with age by the fourth century A.D. Our remote forefathers decorated their houses with evergreens at the Winter Solstice, and lit bonfires in high places to strengthen the reviving sun in his course. During the Saturnalia, candles and green wreaths were given as presents, and the streets were crowded with noisy processions of garlanded men and women carrying lighted tapers. At this festival all distinctions of rank were temporarily forgotten and customary rules of conduct loosened in memory of a golden age of liberty that was supposed to have existed in the far past, when Saturn ruled the world. Masters and servants changed places; slaves wore their owners' clothes and were waited upon by those they normally served, and rich and poor, bond and free joined together as equals in a seven-day round of feasting and drinking, games, dances, masquerades and boisterous frolics of every kind.

The utmost license of speech and action was permitted to all. A mock king was chosen by lot from among the slaves to preside over the revels. As long as his reign lasted, his word was law and his commands had to be obeyed without question by everyone. He could order the performance of ridiculous and undignified antics, deride those in authority, play practical jokes on sober citizens, and generally turn the social order upside down. The wilder his tricks and the more impudent his demands, the better he was esteemed by his temporary subjects. In medieval and Tudor times a somewhat similar part was played by the Lord of Misrule, who was appointed to direct the Christmas festivities in great houses and colleges, and had practically unlimited power over householders and guests during his period of office.

At the Kalends of January, which began on January 1 and lasted for three days, Roman houses were adorned with lights and greenery, and presents, called *strenæ,* were given to friends and children and to the poor. This was the Roman

New Year festival, when divination was practiced to see what the coming year would bring, and even the meanest individual spent money freely on gifts and hospitality. "He who the whole year through has taken pleasure in saving and piling up his pence becomes suddenly extravagant," wrote Libanius in the fourth century, and he adds that it was a virtue of the feast that it taught men not to hold too closely to their money. Men ran about the streets with their faces masked, or dressed in animal skins, with the horns or skulls of animals on their heads. This custom, like the divination already mentioned, was sternly condemned by the Church, but it proved exceedingly difficult to uproot. Many people now living can remember the Hodening Horse and the Christmas Bull, both men disguised as animals, who used to go around at Christmas; and today the Mari Lwyd rite with its decorated horse skull is still observed in South Wales, and guise dancing with blackened faces still survives in some English districts at New Year.

It was the pagan origin of these and other customs which so offended the Puritans in the sixteenth and seventeenth centuries, and gave strength to their attacks upon Christmas itself. During the Commonwealth, when the Puritan party was in power, all celebrations, both religious and secular, were forbidden. The churches were closed and no service was permitted; December 25 was proclaimed an ordinary working day, and those who persisted in treating it as a holy day were fined or imprisoned. With the Restoration, Christmas came into its own again, though some ancient customs had lost a little of their vigor in the interval, and some, like the Lord of Misrule, were already declining toward their end.

In America, or at least in those states which had been first colonized by Puritans, the prejudice was longer lived. In New England Christmas celebrations were forbidden by the authorities in 1659, and although this law was repealed in 1681, sectarian hostility to the feast continued for many years thereafter. Elsewhere, however, and even to some extent in the Puritan colonies, immigrants of other faiths had brought their own customs with them and kept the festival in their new homes as they had done in the old. Gradually their influence and the decline of religious and political bitterness had their effect. One after another the States of the Union acknowledged the importance of Christmas Day by making it a legal holiday, beginning with Alabama in 1836; and by the end of the nineteenth century it was fully accepted everywhere. Today few Americans know that it was ever outlawed in their country, and now Christmas is for them as deeply loved a festival as it is in any other part of Christendom.

2

The Christmas Season

THE ecclesiastical Christmas lasts from Advent until Candlemas and includes a number of lesser feasts, each with its own traditions and customs. If for ordinary people the season is not quite so long, it is certain that Christmas transforms the whole of the early winter, and lends a special light and color to the beginning of the new year. The four weeks of Advent, which immediately precede it, are a time of preparation in both the religious and the secular sense; and for most of us, the traditional Twelve Days between Christmas and Epiphany are still essentially festival days, even though they are no longer the full holidays they once were.

Although Advent depends for its entire meaning upon the great anniversary at its end, it was never without its festal customs, and three important feast days are included in it. In Germany almost every family has its Advent wreath, adorned with small images and four candles, one of which is burned on each of the four Sundays. Around

Berchtesgaden, St. Nicholas, who is also Father Christmas, makes his gift-bringing visits during the first week of Advent, and in Holland and some other European countries he is looked for on the eve of his own feast day, December 6.

During the Middle Ages, St. Nicholas' Day was also the first day of the Boy Bishop's term of office. In cathedrals and choir schools, and in some parish churches, a boy was chosen by his fellow choristers to act as their bishop until Holy Innocents' Day, December 28. This was not a game, but a serious rite. The child bishop performed all the ecclesiastical duties of a real prelate, as far as that was possible, wore episcopal vestments and took the leading part in all Church services, except those which could only be celebrated by an ordained priest. At these services he was supported by other children, whom he had appointed to act as chaplains, canons, and lesser clergy. If he died in office, as one boy did at Salisbury, he was buried with full episcopal honors. On December 28, the last day of his reign, he preached a sermon and went in solemn procession to bless the people. There were other processions also, during which gifts were given to the children by all and sundry, and pleasant entertainments of various kinds which must have seemed especially delightful at that period, when school life was hard and holidays, in the modern sense, very few and short.

However strange the Boy Bishop ceremonies may seem to us now, there is no doubt that they were genuinely religious in conception and execution, and were reverently and efficiently performed by all concerned. They were suppressed by Henry VIII in 1542, and though temporarily revived in Mary I's reign, they disappeared again after that queen's death. They lasted somewhat longer on the Continent, but as ideas changed, they gradually became debased and meaningless, and finally ceased in the eighteenth century. In our own day the ancient custom has been revived in some English and European churches, though in a much modified form, and without the celebration of services by the Boy Bishop, which was so distinctive a feature of the medieval rite.

The great Advent festival in Sweden is St. Lucia's Day, December 13, which is sometimes called Little Yule. This is first and foremost a feast of lights, and its customs probably have very little connection with the real St. Lucia, who was martyred at Syracuse in the fourth century A.D. But her anniversary was also the day of the Winter Solstice, according to the unreformed calendar, and it is this fact which gives its special character to the feast.

Every Swedish parish and village has its Lucia Queen or Lucia Bride, who is dressed in white and wears a crown of lighted candles on her head.

Early in the morning, while it is still dark, she sets out, bearing a tray of food and coffee, to visit houses and farmsteads, cow byres and stables, and so bring a symbolic promise of coming light and plenty to humans and animals alike. With her goes a man on horseback and a long procession of young people who carry burning candles and are variously dressed as maids of honor, "star boys," Biblical characters and trolls and demons defeated by the reviving sun. In many homes also there is a Lucia Queen, usually the youngest daughter, who goes around the house before sunrise, wearing her candle crown and wakening her sleeping family with coffee and songs. Later in the morning, there is a special breakfast in a brightly lit room, and extra rations are given to any animals owned by the household, so that they, too, may share in the rejoicings.

St. Thomas is another Winter Solstice saint, for his feast falls on December 21. This, like Shrove Tuesday, was one of the anniversaries on which schoolboys were formerly allowed to "bar out the master" if they could reach the schoolhouse first. The doors were barricaded, and the master's attempts to force them vigorously resisted. If he managed to get in, he could impose especially heavy tasks on the defeated children; but probably his efforts were never very strenuous, since teachers enjoy holidays quite as much as pupils. Within living memory, women went "Thomassing" or "curning" on December 21, going from house to house to collect gifts of wheat or flour, with which to make a Christmas batch of bread and cakes. Most householders gave a quart or a pint, and received in return a sprig of holly or mistletoe which was supposed to bring good luck. Poor people, who also went gleaning after harvest, often collected enough in these two ways to keep them in flour for most of the winter. Nowadays, when extreme poverty is happily less common, the custom has died out, but a number of fixed charities are still distributed on St. Thomas' Day, so that the recipients may enjoy their Christmas in full measure.

All these Advent customs are, as it were, heralds announcing what is to come. True Christmas begins at midnight on December 24, when Midnight Mass is sung in countless Roman Catholic and High Anglican churches, and the Crib, with its figures of the Holy Family, the animals and the shepherds, is solemnly blessed. In earlier centuries the holiday that followed lasted for twelve days, ending at Epiphany, which we still call Twelfth-day or, more usually, Twelfth-night. This was the period known as the Twelve Days of Christmas, though if Epiphany itself is included, there were actually thirteen days during which little or no work was done and many customary regulations were relaxed. Our modern notions are less generous, and most people now have to be content with a far shorter period of freedom. Yet in spite of all this, the Twelve Days still have a holiday character and are quite unlike any others in the year. While they last, our rooms are filled with greenery and Christmas trees glow with light in private houses, streets and churches. The gifts we have received are still fresh and delightful; parties and pantomimes fill the evening hours; and over the world's horizon a new year is rising, with new hopes and opportunities, and the happy sound of bells.

After Twelfth-night, decorations are normally taken down and Christmas trees dismantled; though if anyone wished to do so, it would be quite correct to keep them until Candlemas Eve. With their disappearance, life puts on its worka-day dress again, except for a few late celebrations which remind us that the Christmas season is not quite over. One of these is Plow Monday, and its eve, Plow Sunday. The Monday after Epiphany once marked the return to farm work after the Twelve Days, and was itself a festival on which certain ancient rituals connected with plowing were observed. Plows were blessed and decorated and were drawn around the village by young men calling themselves Plow-stots or Plow-bullocks. Sword dances were performed—that is, folk dances in which men carry swords and weave them together into a complicated pattern called "the Lock" or "the Rose." Then, too, came the Plow Monday Play, which is akin to the Christmas Mumming Play. Sword dances, and occasionally the Play, are still performed now in northern England, though not in working hours and not always by farm-laborers. The blessing continues also, but on Plow Sunday. In many English parishes a plow is brought into church during the evening service, and there, while farmers and plowmen from many local farms stand around it, the celebrant blesses it and them, and through them, all the agricultural work of the year that has just begun.

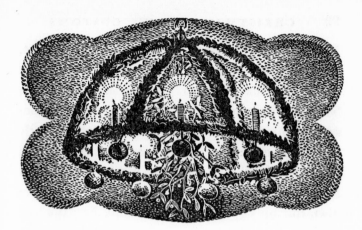

3

Garlands and Greenery

EVERGREENS, which flourish when all else is brown and dead, are obvious symbols of enduring life, and consequently they have always been associated with midwinter festivals. Our primitive forefathers brought in green branches at the Winter Solstice, and used them in magical rites to ensure the return of vegetation. Roman houses were decorated with laurel and bay at the Kalends of January, and for many centuries now, Christian homes and churches have burst into greenery at Christmas time. It is true that the early Church forbade the custom, as savoring of paganism, but it was too deeply rooted

21

for such prohibitions to have permanent effect, and in due course they were annulled or forgotten. "Against the time of Christmas," wrote John Stow in the sixteenth century, "every man's house, as also their parish churches, were decked with holme, ivie, bayes, and whatsoever the season afforded to be greene"; and if he could return to Earth today, he would find little change.

Holly, ivy and mistletoe are the favorite decorations now, as they were in earlier times. To our ancestors they were strong life-symbols, not only because they are evergreens, but also because, unlike most plants, they bear fruit in winter. By tradition, holly is masculine and ivy feminine, thus both are needed if all in the house are to share in the blessings they imply. Mistletoe, the Golden Bough of classical legend, was held sacred by the Celtic Druids and by the Norsemen, for whom it was the holy and terrible plant which slew Balder, the Sun God. It was once called Allheal, for the double reason that it was used in folk medicine to cure many ills, and was the plant of peace, under which enemies were reconciled in ancient Scandinavia. It brought good luck and fertility. It protected the house that contained it from witchcraft and was an antidote to poison. Yet unlike holly and ivy, it never quite lost its heathen character and, though freely used in private households, it was never included in the Christmas decorations of churches. Even today it is rarely found among them, and formerly, if any was accidentally introduced, it was immediately thrown out. The one English exception to this rule was at York Minster, where, during the Middle Ages, a branch was ceremonially laid upon the high altar on Christmas Eve, after which a general pardon and liberty for all was proclaimed throughout the city for so long as it remained there.

Kissing under the mistletoe seems to be a purely English custom, never found in other countries unless Englishmen have settled there. Its survival in its native land may be due to the fact that the English were formerly much given to kissing. Foreign visitors in Tudor and early Stuart times frequently remarked how men and women exchanged kisses without self-consciousness, even slight acquaintances or strangers just introduced being greeted in this pleasant manner. "Wherever you go," wrote Erasmus in the sixteenth century, "everyone welcomes you with a kiss, and the same on bidding farewell . . . in short, turn where you will, there are kisses, kisses everywhere." It need hardly be said that this is no longer the case; but where mistletoe hangs, a shadow of the old freedom reappears. Girls who stand under it cannot refuse to be kissed, and those who dislike such attentions must take care to keep away from the bough.

The lovely custom of lighting and decorating small trees at Christmas came originally from Germany. No one knows how or when it began there. One legend connects it with St. Boniface, who came from England in the eighth century to convert the heathen Germans. He cut down a sacred oak at Geismar one Christmas Eve, and is said to have offered the outraged pagans a young fir tree in its place, to be a symbol of the new faith he preached. A later story says Martin Luther introduced the custom by using a candlelit tree as an image of the starry heavens from which Christ came. This suggests that Christmas trees existed in the sixteenth century; and we know from an anonymous manuscript of 1605 that they were established in Strasbourg then, for the writer records that the citizens set up little fir trees in their parlors and decorated them with paper roses, apples and sweets.

Because of its traditional connection with Luther, the custom was mainly confined to Protestant districts during the seventeenth and eighteenth centuries. From thence it spread slowly over Europe, though it was never as popular in Latin countries as elsewhere. It reached America before it came to England. Hessian soldiers in George III's army are said to have set up Christmas trees during the Revolutionary War, and, earlier still, German settlers in Pennsylvania had their trees, or else the green brushwood pyramids that were used instead of trees in some parts of Germany, candlelit and decorated.

The first English Christmas tree of which we have certain knowledge appeared in 1821, at a children's party given by a member of Queen Caroline's court. Eight years later Princess Lieven, a Russian noblewoman living in London, set up three more for the entertainment of children at Panshanger. In Manchester, where many German merchants had settled, the custom had already spread fast by 1840. William Howitt tells us that pine tops were sold for the purpose in large numbers, and that they were usually lit by as many tapers as there are days in the year, which, if true, must have made a splendid illumination indeed. Then in 1841 the seal of fashion was set upon the new custom, when Prince Albert and Queen Victoria had their first Christmas tree at Windsor Castle. For a little while yet, ordinary people hesitated before adopting what Dickens called "the new German toy"; but within twenty years or so, the Christmas tree was firmly rooted and was slowly but surely taking the place of the older, native Kissing Bough.

This was a hanging garland of greenery, shaped like a double-hooped May garland, or like a

crown, decorated with candles, ornaments, and a
ring of red apples, and having a bunch of mistletoe
suspended from the center. Sometimes small
presents were attached to it by long ribbons. It
hung from the middle of the ceiling, just high
enough to clear the head of the tallest person
present, and for the Twelve Days of Christmas it
was the central point of the festivities. Nowadays
it is less often seen, but it still exists. Some families
never gave it up, and others have readopted it
recently, either as an additional decoration or as
a substitute for the now more usual tree.

Of late years garlands and greenery have come
out of the houses and churches and spread into
the open street. This is not as new a custom as it
appears. Houses were once decorated outside as
well as in, and John Stow tells us that in his day
"the conduits and standardes in the streets were
likewise garnished." Now our shops and public
buildings are decked with lights and real or imita-
tion branches for some time before Christmas.
Many inns hang garlands on their signs or frame
their doorways with colored lamps. In America
holly wreaths tied with red ribbons hang on the
front doors of houses, and this pleasant habit has
now found its way to England. In churches of all
denominations there are Christmas trees, lighted
and decorated, under which anonymous gifts are
heaped for hospitals and orphanages. Usually

these stand in the nave, near the Crib if there is one, or at the west end, but sometimes they are set where all can see them, in the churchyard. At St. Paul's Cathedral there are two, one inside near the west door, and the other outside in the portico. They are the gift of the Queen, and come from her Sandringham estates.

Many towns and villages now have communal trees in their main streets or squares, or on the village green. A communal tree seems so right and natural an expression of the Christmas spirit that it is quite surprising to find the custom is not rooted in antiquity, as might be expected, but is, in fact, quite modern. It belongs by origin to America, though it has now become the cherished possession of many other countries also. In 1909 the people of Pasadena, California, set up an illuminated tree on Mount Wilson. Three years later a similar tree, sixty feet high, appeared in Madison Square Park, New York. Now, since 1933, an enormous illuminated tree in Rockefeller Center, surrounded by the city's most famous group of buildings and shining in the heart of Manhattan, is considered America's most beautiful community tree. The custom of community trees spread through the United States and far beyond it. In England the most famous town tree is that which has come every year since 1947 as Oslo's gift to the citizens of London, and stands in Trafalgar Square under the shadow of Nelson's monument. It is, however, only one among many others which shed their light from Christmas Eve to Epiphany, and are the center of town celebrations and carol-singing. A rather charming extension of the idea of shared rejoicing which underlies these communal trees is sometimes seen in villages or suburbs, where an illuminated tree is placed in some small roadside garden as the householder's unspoken greeting to all who pass by.

4

Fire and Light

CHRISTMAS is essentially a feast of lights and fire. Candles blaze in the churches to remind us that on this night Christ was born, Who is the Light of the World. At home they shine on the Christmas tree and among the decorations on walls and chimney piece, and if in modern houses they are more often electric than waxen, that is only a difference of method and not of underlying conception. Many householders put lighted candles in their windows, a very old custom which sprang originally from the lovely notion that thereby the Christ Child might be guided through the darkness to the house. In medieval times no stranger drawn by their gleam was ever turned away, for who knew whether he might not be Christ Himself, seeking hospitality? In some families a little model of the Christmas Crib is made and placed on a table in the living room, and before this also lighted candles usually stand.

Within living memory, chandlers and grocers used to send gifts of candles to their customers at this season. The true Christmas or Yule Candle is rarely seen now, but it was still well known in the latter half of the last century. It was very large, as it had to burn throughout Christmas Day; if it went out prematurely or was accidentally blown out, it foretold bad luck in the coming year. In Scandinavia it was lit on Christmas Eve and extinguished the next day at sunrise or in some districts just before the hour of morning service. In Denmark two great candles were used, one for the master and the other for the mistress of the house. In Norway the candle extinguished on Christmas morning was lit again each evening until New Year's Day, and in Ireland it burned on Twelfth-night also. It was generally considered unlucky to touch it after it was lit, and the ritual of putting it out was usually done only by the head of the household, or by the oldest member of the family present.

As long as fires burned on great open hearths, the Yule Log played a prominent part in the festivities of many European countries. It was brought in with ceremony on Christmas Eve and kindled with a piece of last year's log, carefully saved for this purpose. Sometimes it was decorated with greenery and ribbons; in Provence wine was poured over it before it was lit, and elsewhere wheat or unleavened bread was placed on it. It was, of course, considered very unlucky if the log did not burn for the whole Twelve Days. In some places the remnant was kindled again on Candlemas Day, and then put out and kept as a charm against fire and lightning. A portion always had to be preserved for next year's log, so that continuity of blessing might be maintained from one year to the next.

Modern fireplaces do not permit the use of Yule Logs, though occasionally a decorated billet is burned on Christmas Day in memory of the old custom. In Devon and Somerset the Ashen Faggot is still brought in on Christmas Eve and lit, like the Yule Log, from a fragment of its predecessor. It is composed of ash sticks bound together by nine ash or withy bands. In private houses these bands are often named for the girls of the family; the one whose band is the first to break will be the first to marry. In inns where the Ashen Faggot appears the same keen interest is taken in the breaking of the first band but for a different reason, for by custom it is the signal for a round of free drinks.

In Colorado a form of Yule Log ceremony was revived in 1934, and has been celebrated regularly at Palmer Lake ever since. A log in the woods is notched and hidden beforehand. On the Sunday before Christmas a bugle calls the people to the town hall, where carols are sung; after which hunters in red and green caps set off to find the hidden log which, when found, is dragged back by ropes— the man who finds it having the right to ride upon it. It is then burned with due ritual in a large stone fireplace, specially built for it, while songs are sung and the wassail bowl is passed around. Here, as elsewhere, part of the log is always saved to kindle next year's brand.

Snapdragon and games with lighted candles are less popular now than they once were, but the Christmas pudding still comes to the table in a blaze of blue, brandy-fed flames. Firecrackers, with their flash and bang, are fire symbols also, though they are not always recognized as such. Around Berchtesgaden young men band themselves into groups for the purpose of firing guns on Christmas Eve. At three o'clock in the afternoon, and again at eleven o'clock at night, they gather on the mountain slopes and, standing in long lines, fire heavy pistols or specially made mortars, either all together or in rapid sequence. Guns are also fired during Midnight Mass, particularly at the Elevation. All this is done now to honor Christ's birth, though probably, like the Twelfth-night firing through apple trees in Somerset, it was once intended to awaken sleeping vegetation and drive away evil spirits.

A very lovely fire custom remains among Syrian Christians. On Christmas Eve the outer gates are locked, in memory of earlier days of persecution, and the whole family, carrying lighted candles, stands around an unlit bonfire in the courtyard. The youngest son then reads the Gospel story, after which the father lights the bonfire. Particular attention is paid to the flames, for on the way they spread depends the luck of the house in the coming year. While the fire burns, psalms are sung, and when it sinks, all leap over the embers, wishing as they do so. Early on Christmas morning, while it is still dark, everyone goes to Mass in the Syrian Church. Here another bonfire is lit in the middle of the floor, and while the dry wood blazes fiercely, ancient hymns are sung, and the celebrant carries a figure of the Christ Child around the building. After the Elevation, he leans over the altar rails and touches the nearest person with his joined hands. This, the Touch of Peace, is passed from one to another till all in the congregation have received it, and then the service continues in the normal manner to its conclusion.

In New Mexico small fires are lit on Christmas Eve outside the houses of Spanish-American families, and lighted candles, fixed in sand-filled paper bags, adorn the roofs and walls. Bonfires blaze at this season in many Scottish parishes also, but these belong to New Year's Eve and Day rather than to Christmas itself. In Wales during the nineteenth century, young men bearing flaming torches used to escort the minister from his house to the four o'clock service on Christmas morning. It was then the custom for Welsh congregations to assemble in church during the small hours and, after hearing a sermon, to sing psalms and hymns until daybreak. Those who for any reason were unable to be present observed the same rite at home. This service, for which the church was lit by colored candles, was known as *Plygain,* or the Crowing of the Cock.

Nowadays *Plygain,* if it is held at all, occurs more often on New Year's morning, but in Norway a somewhat similar service, called *Julotte,* still takes place at Christmas. There, too, the people wait for the dawn in the parish church, which is brilliantly lit by rows of candles fixed to the backs of the benches. The Moravian Christmas Eve service at Bethlehem, Pennsylvania, is also associated with waiting and with candlelight, but it begins on the evening of December 24 and culminates at midnight. Candles are everywhere about the church, and each person present receives a beeswax taper in a holder especially made for the occasion, which he carries while carols and songs are sung. This custom is said to have started in 1741 at the Moravian settlement at Herrnhut. In that year Count von Zinzendorf, leader of the European Moravians, took a lighted candle in his hand and led his followers into the stable, there to keep their Christmas vigil with hymns and prayers and Bible readings, as their descendants now do in the Pennsylvania church.

5

Gifts and Greetings

THE exchange of gifts and greetings at or near Christmas time began long before Christianity gave a new and deeper meaning to the custom. In pagan Rome rich men gave generously to their poorer neighbors during the Saturnalia and received garlands or tapers or grains of frankincense in return. Small clay or paste images were specially made at this season and given to children. At the Kalends of January gifts were even more plentiful. In the beginning these New Year presents, or *strenæ,* are said to have been simple boughs of greenery brought from the groves of the goddess Strenia, but as time went on they became more elaborate. Many were charms as well as gifts. Men gave one another "honeyed things," so that the recipient might be sure of sweetness in the coming year; lamps, so that he might have light and warmth; and money, or gold and silver objects, so that he might have increasing wealth. We still see a shadow of this ancient idea in the symbolic gifts of the First-foot in Scotland and northern England. When Libanius wrote in the fourth century, these happy exchanges were common all over the Roman Empire, and in his lively account of the New Year festival, he tells us that "as the thousand flowers which burst forth everywhere are the adornment of Spring, so are the thousand presents poured out on all sides the decoration of the Kalends feast."

Because gift-giving was so essential a part of the pagan celebrations, the early Church frowned upon it as sternly as upon other and more questionable New Year customs. In the first centuries, Christians did not give each other presents in the Christmas season, or if they did, it was without ecclesiastical sanction. Yet it is hard to believe that so ancient and charming a habit was altogether abandoned, and, in fact, there is a good deal of evidence that it was not. For the devout believer it must always have seemed a natural expression of rejoicing to give generously to kinsfolk and the poor at this holy time, and thereby to commemorate the splendid gifts of the Magi to the Infant Jesus, and those humbler presents, which the shepherds are traditionally said to have laid before the manger on the first Christmas Day. However that may be, we know that New Year gifts never quite died out in Europe, and by the twelfth century the giving of presents on the day or eve of the Nativity was already becoming usual.

In some countries where Latin influence was strong, January 1 has remained the principal present-giving date. In France young children put their sabots in the hearth for the Christ Child to fill, but adults normally exchange gifts at New Year. In Sweden presents are sometimes given on St. Lucia's Day, and in Spain and Italy on Epiphany Eve. In Holland most families have a Christmas tree at the usual time, but only fruit and sweets are hung among its candles and decorations; the real presents are distributed three weeks earlier, on St. Nicholas' Eve.

In England until quite recently, postmen, dustmen and other public servants came round on Boxing Day, December 26, to receive their Christmas boxes, or small gifts of money, from the householders they served during the year. This custom is fast dying out now, as ideas change and wages rise, but formerly it was very general, and sprang from a real desire to share the joys of Christmas with all who were even remotely connected with the giver's family. At one time the circle of beneficiaries was far wider than it subsequently became. Not postmen and dustmen only, but lamplighters, turncocks, errand boys, apprentices and journeymen expected their Christmas boxes, and they were rarely disappointed. In Scotland similar payments were made on Handsel Monday, the first Monday of the new year. In some parishes the clergyman was expected to provide bread, cheese and ale for his parishioners, and on many farms great pies were cut up on Boxing Day morning and sent round to the farmer's laborers.

The origin of the name "Boxing Day" is obscure. Some think it is derived from the alms boxes in parish churches which were opened, and their contents distributed to the needy, on the day after Christmas. Others believe it to be connected with the earthenware boxes which apprentices carried when collecting money from their master's customers. Whatever the true explanation may be, it is certain that the title is now so common in England that many people are in danger of forgetting the real name of December 26, which is, of course, St. Stephen's Day.

St. Stephen, the first Christian martyr, was traditionally connected with horses, though why this should be so is not clear. There is nothing in his legend to account for the association, and it seems probable that he inherited it from earlier pagan rituals of the season, or borrowed it from a later Swedish saint of the same name who was reputed to love horses. In several North European countries ceremonial rides and horse races took place on December 26, and in some, including England, horses were bled then to preserve their health. It is still customary in fox-hunting districts for a meet to be held on Boxing Day, often in the market square of a small country town or outside some great house, but though many fine horses are to be seen on such occasions, it would perhaps be stretching the theory of survival too far to connect them with St. Stephen. In larger towns the principal excitement of the day is the opening of the pantomime season, or rather it was, for of recent years many theaters have started their pantomimes on other dates. It is still the accepted time for the first appearance of the Christmas Mummers, in those country areas where the ancient Mumming Play has survived. This is a folk play, symbolizing the sowing and growth of the corn, in which one of the characters is killed during a fight, and is afterward magically brought to life again.

Christmas cards, which are now sent out in millions every year, are little more than a century old. Their immediate predecessors were the "Christmas pieces" which schoolboys produced, reluctantly enough, no doubt, at the end of the winter term. These were sheets of paper specially made for the purpose, with colored borders and headings, on which the boys wrote, in careful copperplate, sentences which served at once as greetings to their parents and proof of their progress in the art of writing. Slightly more elaborate sheets of the same type were sometimes used by adults for complimentary verses and polite messages, to send with a gift or letter. But this type of greeting was by no means common, and it was not until the fourth decade of the nineteenth century that the true Christmas card came into being.

The actual date is uncertain, and so is the identity of the inventor, for more than one person has laid claim to the honor. A card designed by a boy named William Egley, and now in the British Museum, may have appeared as early as 1842, but, unfortunately, the date under his signature is not clear, and the last figure might be either a 2 or a 9. In 1844 lithographed greetings were sent out by the Reverend Edward Bradley of Newcastle, and in the same year W. A. Dobson, then head of the School of Design in Birmingham, used hand-painted cards to save himself the trouble of writing letters. The strongest claim to inventor is, however, that of J. C. Horsley, an artist who, in 1843, designed a pictorial card with a Christmas greeting on it at the suggestion of Sir (then Mr.) Henry Cole. In his old age, Horsley gave 1846 as the date of the card, but this must have been due to forgetfulness, for he himself sent out one with 1843 clearly on it, and thus (if Egley's claim is rejected) firmly established himself as the pioneer of the new fashion.

About a thousand copies were sold, the first small trickle of what was later to be a steady stream and eventually a torrent. By 1870 Christmas cards were well established in England, and a few years later they reached the United States. The early designs were simple and pleasant, gradually becoming more elaborate as time went on. In the eighties, many were really beautiful, and almost all were appropriate to the season. Nowadays there is an unfortunate tendency to use designs that are entirely irrelevant to Christmas, which, as Lawrence Whistler remarks in his charming book, *The English Festivals,* "is bad festival manners." No doubt the wish for novelty and variety is the mainspring of this habit, but Christmas has, after all, a unique character of its own which is hardly suggested by pictures of summer sports, reproductions of old maps, and even battle scenes.

One modern design, however, extremely popular in the United States and Canada, has its own special interest. This involves the Poinsettia, which of late years has become an accepted Christmas emblem in North America. Its lovely scarlet color makes it truly at home in the festival of fire and light, and evidently it was considered so before Dr. Poinsett discovered it in 1828, for its Mexican name was Flower of the Holy Night. Today the living blossom is given as a present and included in decorations all over North America, and pictures of it appear on millions of Christmas cards and on the acres of ornamental paper and miles of ribbon used every year in the wrapping of gifts.

6

The Gift-bringer

CHRISTMAS gifts are never quite the same as those given at other times of the year because, almost everywhere, they are associated with a gift-bringer who, whether he is Father Christmas or St. Nicholas or the Three Kings or Knight Rupprecht, is always someone mysterious and shadowy, outside the run of ordinary human experience. His home is far away in Heaven or at the North Pole or in some remote country from which he comes on horseback, or in a sleigh drawn by reindeer. He may come secretly by night, or openly in the winter daylight, accompanied by a train of masked demons and strange animal forms. Often he is associated with fire, entering the house by the chimney, or leaving his gifts by the hearth. In the older form of the legend he is always two-sided, coming not only to reward the good but also to punish the bad. He can distinguish between the two, because, like the ancient gods from whom he is descended, he can read the heart and knows the hidden thoughts and actions of those he visits. This aspect of his character is now almost entirely forgotten in England and America, where Father Christmas (or Santa Claus) is altogether benevolent, but in many European countries it is well remembered and has its clear effects upon the local customs.

In England Father Christmas changed his outward form, though not his essential nature, during the nineteenth century, but he was known and loved long before that time. There is a fifteenth-century carol which begins "Hail Father Christmas, hail to thee!" He is one of the characters in many versions of the country Mumming Play, which is far older than the carol. He appeared in Tudor and Stuart court masques; and in the mid-seventeenth century one writer described him as that "old, old, very old graybearded gentleman called Christmas, who was wont to be a very familiar guest and visit all sorts of people, both poor and rich." That was written during the dark period, beginning in 1644, when the Puritan

Parliament forbade all festival observances, whether these were religious services or popular junketings. Father Christmas was then driven underground, but he continued to exist, and he returned in triumph with Charles II. He was not in this early manifestation primarily a gift-bringer, but rather Christmas itself, with all that meant in the way of rejoicing and plenty. Then, in the Victorian era, when the German Christmas tree first appeared, he, too, took on a Teutonic character, and eventually he became what he is today, the night rider in a reindeer-drawn sleigh, descender of chimneys, and the supreme bringer of gifts for children everywhere.

He is still, however, an "old, old, very old gray-bearded gentleman," and this is as it should be, for his age is immense. Once he was Odin, who rode through the midwinter world on his eight-footed horse, Sleipnir, bringing reward or punishment; and behind the Norse god there are glimpses of earlier, mistier spirits of the Winter Solstice and the reviving earth. But when Christianity drove away the old gods, he remained, and appeared again as St. Nicholas, who was Bishop of Myra in the fourth century, and afterwards became the patron saint of children and sailors.

The transformation was easy because the bishop was renowned while he lived for his great generosity and his love of children. Legend says he once miraculously restored to life three school-boys who had been murdered by an innkeeper. On another occasion, hearing that a man in Patara, his native town, was about to sell his dowerless daughters into prostitution because of bitter poverty, he saved the girls by dropping bags of gold secretly through their window, and so providing them with sufficient marriage portions. Other poor people often found his anonymous gifts slipped into their houses by night just when they needed them most. All these stories, and the fact that his feast day fell within the Christmas season, made it almost inevitable that the kindly saint should posthumously acquire some of the attributes of the ancient gift-bringer; and as the years passed, he gradually changed in popular tradition from the human bishop, who had once lived and now was dead, to that mysterious immortal being known to us as Santa Claus.

In Europe the fact that he was a bishop is more clearly remembered than it is in England or America. In Holland, Switzerland and parts of Germany and Austria, he is represented by a man dressed in episcopal robes and miter, who appears on St. Nicholas' Eve (December 5) or on Christmas Eve, and sometimes preaches a short sermon, or makes the children recite their catechism, before he distributes the presents. In Holland he comes from Spain on St. Nicholas' Eve, riding on a white horse and accompanied by a black servant, who carries the gifts. Dutch children put their clogs in the hearth and fill them with hay and sugar for the horse; in the morning both are gone, and the clogs are filled with sweetmeats. When St. Nicholas appears in person, he shows a disconcertingly intimate knowledge of recent childish misdemeanors, and if a child has been very bad, there is some talk of putting him into the servant's sack and carrying him off to Spain. But somehow this never actually happens, and when the Saint's little homily is ended, the distribution of presents proceeds without further alarms.

Here the black servant (supposedly a Moor from Spain) may be the last survivor in Holland of that train of strange creatures who often accompany St. Nicholas in other lands. Probably they were fertility spirits originally but now they are demons. In some Alpine regions the bishop's way is cleared by two "ghosts of the field," swathed in straw from head to foot, and lashing all round them with heavy whips. After them come a man with a goat's head, and a masked and horned creature of demonic appearance who carries a birch. These two are there to chastise sinners, especially women, outside whose houses the goat bleats. Nowadays this is just a frolic, but there can be little doubt that it once had a serious ritual meaning. Finally the bishop arrives, with his gift-bearing servant, and the demons disappear.

In the Berchtesgaden district of Bavaria, St. Nicholas visits the houses during the first week of Advent, attended by a boy dressed as a girl, who is called the *Nikolo-Weibl,* and twelve *Butten-mandln.* These last are young men dressed in straw, with animal masks or skins over their heads, and large cowbells tied about them, with which they make a loud and terrifying noise. At each house the bishop makes a short religious speech, and the *Nikolo-Weibl* distributes gifts; then both withdraw, and the *Buttenmandln* fall upon the young people in the room and drive them out with shouts and blows. Sometimes quite rough handling has to be endured, but no one minds, for the *Buttenmandln* are luck-bringers and their blows, though now explained as punishments for idleness or bad behavior, derive in fact from pre-Christian fertility ceremonies by which good fortune and plenty were once ensured for all.

Elsewhere in central and northern Europe St. Nicholas may be accompanied by St. Peter or the Archangel Gabriel or by Knight Rupprecht. The last-named, whose origin is very obscure, often comes alone and is a gift-bringer in his own right. He wears skins or straw, and has a very fierce appearance. In some districts he is called *ru-Klas,* or rough Nicholas, which suggests that he may be an older pagan spirit, to whom the saint's name has been lent to make him slightly more respectable in Christian eyes. By some he is identified with Odin; but if he started life as a heathen god, he is careful now to examine North German children in Christian prayers, and to punish them if their knowledge proves faulty. When the first German settlers went to Pennsylvania, he went with them, and he is still remembered there (though now rarely seen) as Belsnickel, servant of St. Nicholas, who represented the darker side of that gentle saint's character.

In Spain presents are given at Epiphany, and it is the Three Kings who bring them. Spanish tradition says that the Wise Men ride every year to Bethlehem on Epiphany Eve, and formerly companies of men used to go out with torches and bells to look for them. Children put their shoes out on the window sill, or on the balcony, in the certain hope that the Kings will fill them as they ride past, and beside the shoes a little straw is left for the benefit of the horses. Epiphany is the great present-giving season in Italy also, but here it is Befana, a female spirit of uncertain lineage, who is the gift-bringer. Little is known about her. Even her name is uninformative, for it is clearly derived from that of the festival with which she is connected. That she is pre-Christian is suggested by the fact that naughty children are often warned she will carry them away and eat them if they do not reform. Yet, notwithstanding this ogrelike side of her character, her coming is eagerly awaited every year, and in Florence formerly it was celebrated with processions and bonfires, and much blowing of trumpets in the streets.

In France it is sometimes Father Christmas and sometimes the Infant Jesus who fills the sabots left in the hearth on Christmas Eve. In Westphalia it is to the Christ Child—*Das Christkind*—that letters of request are written a little before Christmas, and left on the window sill for Him to read. On December 24 a table is set between the Christmas tree and the open window, and on it soup plates, one for each child, are arranged. In the morning these plates are found to be full of sweets and fruits, and more important presents are piled on the table. *Christkind* has come and gone, though no one has seen Him. In Alsace, however, He has a human representative in the rather unexpected form of a girl wearing a candle crown, like the Lucia Queen, and carrying a silver bell in one hand and a basket of gifts in the other. She is called *Christkind,* but she bears little resemblance to the Holy Child, for not only is she of the wrong sex and age, but she is also accompanied by a figure from the heathen past—

the terrible demon, Hans Trapp, who, dressed in a bearskin and having a blackened face, threatens all naughty children with his wildly brandished stick until *Christkind* intervenes and saves them.

Perhaps the most mysterious of all the traditional gift-bringers is he (or she) who brings the *Julklapp* in Sweden and the northernmost provinces of Germany. *Julklapp* is a gift done up in many wrappings, so cunningly arranged that it is difficult to find the actual object. He who brings it must come unexpectedly and unannounced. He flings open the door, throws in the gift, and vanishes with the utmost speed. It is essential that he come and go before anyone has time to see or recognize him. Occasionally, the *Julklapp* is brought by two masked figures dressed as an old man and an old woman, the first carrying a bell which he rings outside the house, and the second a basket of presents. Here, too, the givers, though they are seen, are unrecognizable. This insistence on a kind of token invisibility is very interesting, and it does not seem clear who or what the unseen donor represents. Can it be that we are back again with Odin, the ancient gift-bringer, still going invisibly about at Yuletide, as in past centuries, through the lands where he was once supreme?

7

The Christmas Feast

"FOR Food and Fellowship, Thank God," says the simplest of all graces, and of these two blessings there has never been any lack at Christmas time. A vast dinner of roast turkey, with all its trimmings, plum pudding and mince pies appears every year on countless tables throughout the English-speaking world, even in those parts of it, such as Australia, where Christmas comes in the heat of summer. Yet turkey, though now traditional, is a comparative newcomer, unknown in Europe before about 1542, and appearing then only as one among a variety of festival dishes. Goose or beef or Christ-

mas pies with many ingredients were the earlier
favorites in ordinary families, while in great
houses there were bustards, swans, venison, pea-
cocks with their tails spread and their beaks
gilded, and chief over all, the boar's head.

This last has a long lineage. It was eaten during
the Scandinavian Yule in honor of the Sun-boar.
The heroes of Valhalla were believed to feast con-
tinually on boar's flesh, and the animal itself was
sacred to Celt and Norseman alike. At the great
medieval Christmas banquets the head was garlanded with rosemary and bay, and an orange or
an apple was thrust between the teeth. It was
brought in with ceremony to the sound of trumpets, slowly borne in upon a gold or silver dish
by the chief cook, and accompanied by a procession of minstrels and servants. This custom is still
observed at The Queen's College, Oxford, where
the decorated head is carried on a silver basin by
four men, preceded by the chief singer, and followed by a choir singing the refrain of the ancient
Boar's Head Carol. Three times the procession
halts, while a verse of the carol is sung by the
chief singer, and finally the head is placed upon
the high table, where the orange from its mouth
is presented to the singer, and the sprigs of rosemary and bay are distributed among the guests.

Such splendid dishes as these belonged to the
era of the open hearth and the swinging cauldron,

the roasting spit and the vast side ovens built into
the walls of spacious kitchens. So, too, did the
enormous Christmas pie, containing quantities of
different birds and sometimes needing, like that
made for Sir Henry Grey in 1770, two bushels of
flour and twenty pounds of butter for the pastry.
There is no room for them now in the modern
household, nor, alas, for the lavish hospitality that
made them necessary. But the mince pie beloved
by our sixteenth-century ancestors is still with us,
and so is the pleasant superstition that whoever
eats one such pie on each of the Twelve Days will
have twelve happy months in the following year.
Christmas puddings, as we know them today, date
only from about 1670, and began as a stiffened
form of the earlier plum porridge. This was made
of meat broth, chopped neats' tongues, raisins,
fruit juice, wine and spices, thickened by bread-
crumbs and served in a semiliquid state. Another
once popular dish was furmenty, made of wheat
slowly stewed in milk, with raisins, sugar and
spices. In some English country districts it was
always the first food eaten on Christmas morning,
as ale posset was the last drink taken on the previous night.

The ceremonial Christmas drink today is often
punch, but formerly it was lambswool. This was
a mixture of hot ale, sugar, spices, eggs and roasted
apples, to which thick cream was sometimes added,

and sippets of toast or French bread. It was served
in a huge wassail bowl, like that owned by Jesus
College, Oxford, which is silver gilt and holds ten
gallons. Humbler bowls of the same festive kind
were carried round during the Twelve Days by
young men singing the ancient carol that begins:

"Wassail! Wassail! all over the town,

Our toast it is white, our ale it is brown,"
and goes on to invoke blessings in turn upon master, mistress, children and all within the house. In
the Shetland Isles a drink made only for the Yule
feast was whipcoll, consisting of egg yolks beaten
with sugar, on to which cream was slowly poured,
the whole being then seasoned with a generous
allowance of rum or brandy.

In Catholic countries where the vigil of Christmas is a fast day, and also in Scandinavia, fish is
the principal item of the Christmas Eve supper.
Stewed eels are popular in Italy, and elsewhere
carp, or herring salad, is eaten, or dried cod
soaked in lyewater and served with a special sauce.
A traditional Danish dessert for this supper is
creamy rice, flavored with spices and a liberal ad-
mixture of raisins and candied fruits.

In Poland the meal which ends the day-long
fast of Wigilia, or Christmas Eve, begins when the
first star appears in the sky, and consists of soup,
fish of various kinds, cabbage, mushrooms and
sweetmeats made from honey and poppy seeds.

The master of the house first distributes small pieces of unleavened bread to every member of the family and carries some to the horses and cattle in the outbuildings. Then everyone sits down to a table on which a white cloth covers a layer of straw or hay, in memory of Christ's birth in a stable. In some houses a wheat sheaf stands in each corner of the room, and later these sheaves are taken into the orchard, where they serve both as a charm to ensure a plentiful fruit harvest and a feast for countless birds.

The charming custom of sharing Christmas plenty with animals and birds is observed in many European countries. Cattle and horses are given extra rations of their own food, and a little of whatever they are likely to enjoy from their master's table, including ale for the horses. Silesian peasants sometimes carry wheat to church on Christmas Day, and afterwards give it to the poultry as a protection against evil. In Sweden a sheaf of corn is often laid on a wheel on top of a high pole for the wild birds, or small handfuls are set on the roof or along garden walls. In South Germany also, corn is strewn on the housetops, and in some parts of Hungary the last sheaf of harvest is, or used to be, kept for a bird feast on New Year's Day. There is no doubt that these excellent customs are very old, rooted alike in natural kindliness and ancient magic; and in the thirteenth

century St. Francis of Assisi gave them added
meaning when he taught that the animal world
should be included in the rejoicings, "for reverence of the Son of God Whom on such a night the
most Blessed Virgin Mary did lay down in the
stall between the ox and the ass."

The games of Christmas Day are old, too,
though some wear modern dress. Snapdragon,
with its dish of burning brandy out of which
raisins must be snatched quickly enough to avoid
scorched fingers, was known long ago, and if our
crackers and indoor fireworks are new, they are
only a modern form of the ancient fire games
played at this season. The Lord of Misrule has
vanished, but if he could return, he would instantly recognize our paper caps and crowns, our
charades and "dressing-up" games. Blindman's
Buff and Nuts in May were known in the Middle
Ages, and so were the quieter games played with
roasted nuts and apples to divine the future,
though these rightly belong to New Year, or to
Hallowe'en, which was once the Celtic New Year's
Eve.

For the British all over the world Christmas
Day is now highlighted by the Queen's speech.
It was King George V who first spoke to his people over the radio on Christmas Day, 1932, and
every year thereafter, and the custom has been
carried on by his son and his granddaughter in

their turn. At three o'clock in the afternoon (which may mean a time varying from early morning to late at night for Commonwealth lands far away from England), millions of the Queen's subjects gather around their radios to listen to that well-known voice, which is for them the supreme symbol of unity. The custom, like the machine that makes it possible, is only a few years old, but it is rooted in something that runs back to the very beginnings of kingship and loyalty; and for countless men and women throughout the British Commonwealth of Nations it has already become an essential part of the festival, without which Christmas would not now seem quite complete. The practice of formally inaugurating the season with a speech has also taken hold in the United States, where it is customary for the President to say a few words to the nation when he lights the tree on the White House lawn a day or so before Christmas.

8

Carols

"ON Christmas night all Christians sing, To hear the news the angels bring," says a traditional Sussex carol, and sing they did, from the fourteenth century onwards, in words that were sometimes merry and sometimes tender, but always simple and homely, set to lilting, happy tunes that suggest dance rhythms rather than the music of hymns. The word "carol" originally meant a ring dance accompanied by a song, and this dancing ancestry has never been quite forgotten, as anyone who sings or whistles "I Saw Three Ships Come Sailing In" or "Ding Dong,

Merrily on High," will instantly realize. Such dance songs were mainly secular in theme, concerned with love and courtship, feasting, the return of spring, or any other cheerful matter, and it was not until the end of the thirteenth or beginning of the fourteenth century that the true religious carol was first heard.

Christmas hymns had existed long before, but these were stately Latin verses that dealt with the theological rather than the human aspect of the Incarnation. Carols were not and never have been hymns, though they are sometimes confused with them. They began with the great religious revival led by St. Francis of Assisi, and flowered into full beauty during the three centuries that followed, as gay and lovely expressions of popular belief and joy in mankind's salvation. Their distinguishing note then, as now, was happiness, and that happiness was expressed with a spontaneous vigor that makes even the oldest carol seem as modern and alive today as it was when it was first sung long ago.

Many surviving English carols were composed between 1400 and the middle of the seventeenth century, and so, too, were numerous others in Italy, France, Germany, Spain and elsewhere. In England they fell upon evil times after about 1647. Puritan disapproval drove them out of the churches and the homes of the educated, and even the return of Charles II, which restored so many good things lost during the Commonwealth, did not restore them to their ancient popularity. For two hundred years thereafter they were heard only among simple folk. As late as 1826 William Hone wrote of them in his *Every-day Book* as "ditties which now exclusively enliven the industrious servant maid and the humble labourer," and when Davies Gilbert and William Sandys published their collections of carols in 1822 and 1833 respectively, they believed they were recording something that would soon be altogether extinct.

Yet, though they did not know it, these two men were themselves the first swallows of a returning summer. The folk carol had never quite died out in rural areas, where long memories and printed broadsheets had preserved the ancient texts. During the nineteenth century many of these old songs were collected and published, including, besides the native English examples, some translations from *Piæ Cantiones,* a rare Swedish book compiled in 1582, which contained carols for Eastertide as well as Christmas. Then, when Cecil Sharp began his great work, many fine songs were recovered from the lips of old people who remembered them from their youth. New carols were also being written; and slowly but surely the Christmas carol came out of its long eclipse and became once more an essential part of popular rejoicings, as it had been for our ancestors five hundred years ago.

In the eighteenth century it was often the town Waits who carried these lovely tunes from door to door, lighting their way with lanterns and playing upon wind instruments. Originally the Waits were simply watchmen, who patrolled the streets and called the hours during the night. Later, however, the name was commonly applied to the town musicians who played for processions and civic occasions, and could also be engaged by private citizens for weddings and feasts. At Christmas they "walked the parish" with music, and were suitably rewarded by the householders outside whose homes they played. Toward the end of the eighteenth century many towns abolished their official Waits, but the title lived on for some time as the popular name for any local group of musicians who went around playing or singing at Christmas time. It was one such rustic band which so delighted Washington Irving when he was staying in Yorkshire in 1820. "I had scarcely got into bed," he wrote afterward in his *Sketch Book,*

"when a strain of music seemed to break forth in the air, just below the window. I listened and found it proceeded from a band, which I concluded to be the waits from some neighboring village. They went around the house, playing under the windows. The sounds, as they receded, became more soft and aerial, and seemed to accord with quiet and moonlight."

The Waits have gone now, carrying their oboes, serpents, clarinets and fiddles away with them into the past, but carol-singers still go on their rounds. Sometimes it is a trained choir or a glee club that sings outside the houses in the winter dusk, collecting money for a recognized charity. Or it may be a little group of children seeking a Christmas box, like the Waits before them. Occasionally (but no longer as often as could be wished) it is the hand-bell ringers, whose clear, thin bell notes sound out the old tunes. At one time almost every parish had its ringers who went around with the carolers, or by themselves, and in some places accompanied the Christmas hymns in church. Bell music is still an important part of the English Christmas, but it is more often the pealing of church bells for Christmas Eve and Christmas morning that we think of now than the gentler note of hand bells. At Dewsbury in Yorkshire, the age of the year is rung and the bell tolled just before midnight on December 24. This is known as the Old Lad's Passing Bell, or the Devil's Knell, "because the Devil died when Christ was born."

In many towns there is organized carol-singing, led by the local clergy or the mayor, around the communal Christmas tree. Almost every small club, guild, women's institute and young people's association has its Carol Night at some time during the season, and in 1956 a choir of railwaymen sang for the delight of travelers and others in the great hall of Euston Station in London. In the churches everywhere there are carol services, varying from simple congregational singing to the beautiful Nine Lessons, in which readings from the Gospels alternate with the singing of nine ancient carols. One such Nine Lessons service is broadcast every year from King's College Chapel in Cambridge where, on Chrismas Eve afternoon, a procession of candle-bearing clergy and choristers enters by the west door, and the lovely ritual is conducted by the dim light of candle flames.

On the other side of the world there are "carols by candlelight" also. In Melbourne on Christmas Eve three hundred thousand people gather every year to sing in the riverside Alexandra Gardens with candles in their hands. Thousands of little flames burn in the still, summer air around a great central platform with a Christmas tree on it, all over the gardens, and along both banks of the river. People of every class and faith take part, and at midnight all join hands and sing "Auld Lang Syne" as the bells ring out for Christmas Day. This custom began only twenty years ago, when Norman Banks first thought of it in 1937, after seeing an old lady listening to carol-singing on the radio with a lighted candle in her hand. Now it is a firmly established annual event in Melbourne, and not only there, for the idea has been widely copied in other parts of Australia, and Carols by Candlelight are sung today in towns and villages all over the Commonwealth.

9

The New Year

AS soon as midnight has struck on New Year's morning, a ring of cheerful noise encircles the world. Church bells are pealed, ships sound their sirens and trains their whistles, glasses are raised to toast the newborn year, and good wishes are exchanged everywhere. Complete rationalists may point out that our divisions of time are purely arbitrary, and that this moment is really no different from any other; but complete rationalists are, perhaps fortunately, comparatively rare, and for the great majority of people January 1 brings with it all the magic of a fresh start and a new, untried period of hope and endeavor. Whether the first moments are spent in church, at a Watch Night service, or at some hilarious party, the underlying idea is still the same—the strong hope of better living (in either or both senses of that phrase), and the half-acknowleged feeling that as the beginning is, so will the rest of the year be. Then it is that good resolutions are made again, notwithstanding the depressing experience of previous years; and if attempts at divining the future are less common at New Year's than they once were, other age-old magical rites are still performed, half in fun, or as a matter of custom, but usually with a lurking notion that it would be unlucky to omit them.

In England New Year's gifts have almost disappeared, and the day itself is no longer observed as a holiday, except in a few districts along the Scottish border and around Manchester. Most people, however, celebrate the beginning of the year in some way or other. In London great crowds assemble outside St. Paul's Cathedral to see the old year out, and welcome the new with cheers and the singing of "Auld Lang Syne." Watch Night services are now very usual in Anglican as well as other churches. These are not, as might be supposed, survivals of the medieval past; they were instituted in the eighteenth century by the Methodist Society, and spread from thence to other communions. In a few parishes they end with the beautiful ceremony of singing a hymn on top of the church tower, and in nearly all the New Year is rung in by the pealing of church bells.

In the northern counties, as in Scotland, the First-foot still goes round on his luck-bringing errand as soon after midnight as possible. He must be the first visitor of the year, as his name indicates, and no one should be admitted to the house before he comes. He brings in a piece of coal, a piece of bread and a little money or salt— magical gifts by which he ensures that the families he visits will have warmth, food and wealth throughout the year. Sometimes he carries a branch of evergreen as a symbol of continuing life. At one time he entered the house in silence and walked straight over to the hearth, where he stirred the fire before turning to greet the company. No one spoke until he had done so, for only then had the true luck of the year been brought to the household. This part of the ritual, with its solemn undertones, is now usually forgotten, and in most places today he is noisily welcomed, and greetings are exchanged as soon as he arrives.

The First-foot must always be a man, for a woman as the year's first visitor would be extremely unlucky. He must be dark-haired (except in a few districts where it is equally essential that he should be fair), and he must not be flat-footed. The luckiest of all First-foots is a dark-haired stranger, but since such a man can hardly be relied upon to appear uninvited, at the right moment, a friend usually performs the office, or a particular man of the correct color may arrange to visit every house in a street or village. Where no outsider is available, a dark-haired member of the family sometimes goes out just before the old year ends, and returns after midnight with the necessary gifts in his hand.

Elsewhere the luck is sometimes brought, not by an individual but by companies of mummers or dancers, or bands of singing youths. At St. Ives in Cornwall the guise dancers perform in the streets during the first fortnight in January. Formerly they used to dance through the houses, as the Furry dancers still do at Helston on May 8, and it was considered very unlucky for any household to be left unvisited. In some Polish districts guisers in masks and exotic headdresses act a short and boisterous play on New Year's Eve, and are rewarded with wine and a gift of money. This custom stopped during the last war and the troubled times that followed, but it has now been revived. Once, of course, the guisers went to every house in the parish. Now they go only where they know they will be welcomed, but occasionally they remind the unfriendly of their existence by playing tricks upon them. In Macedonia young lads knock thunderously upon doors with sticks and clubs, and cry their greetings in the early hours of January 1, or, in some parts of the country, they run about with green branches, with which they touch all whom they meet to bring them good fortune. So, too, in South Wales sixty or seventy years ago, children drew "near water" from a well before dawn and sprinkled it over those they met with a sprig of evergreen. They also went round to the houses and woke the sleeping inmates with a very curious and beautiful old carol.

In Scotland, New Year, or Hogmanay, is the great festival of the year, far exceeding Christmas in importance. Many explanations have been suggested for the name "Hogmanay." It has been variously derived by scholars from French, Greek, Norse or Spanish words connected with the season, but no general agreement on the subject has been reached as yet. Whatever the true origin of its name, the feast itself reigns supreme throughout Scotland, and is annually celebrated by cheerful customs and merrymaking.

In Edinburgh enormous crowds gather outside the Tron Church on New Year's Eve, there to wait for midnight. As soon as the clock strikes there is an outburst of shouted good wishes, handshakes, toasts, bonnets flung into the air, and eightsome reels danced to the wild music of bagpipes. At Biggar, and at Wick in the far north, the old year is burnt out with enormous bonfires, round which the people dance, and elsewhere there are midnight parades with torches. At Stonehaven there is a fireball procession in which flaming balls of tallow-coated rope are swung around on the ends of long cords. In some parts of Angus, farmers take their guns just before the clock strikes to "shoot the old year out." Time-honored games are played on New Year's Day in several districts, and special cakes made for children who come round singing old rhymes. And everywhere there is visiting between neighbors, lavish hospitality, and hearty consumption of the traditional foods (and drinks) of the season.

At Burghead, Morayshire, a very interesting and ancient fire-ceremony, known as Burning the Clavie, is performed on January 11, Old New Year's Eve. The Clavie is the bottom half of a tar barrel, filled with tar and wood, and fixed upon a pole called the Spoke by a single long nail specially forged for the purpose. No other metal may be used in its preparation, the nail itself being hammered in with a stone hammer. Only local men are allowed to help in the work, and, when all is ready, the tar-and-wood filling must be lit with a burning peat or brand. No matches or modern lighters are permitted. The flaming Clavie is carried around the old town and up the Doorie Hill by relays of young men, led by the Clavie King, who for several generations now has been a member of the same family. All along the route house doors are left open, so that luck-bringing faggots may be flung through them. On the hilltop the Clavie is fixed on to an ancient stone altar, and fresh tar is poured over it to keep it blazing. When it begins to burn down, it is hacked to pieces by the Clavie King and his followers. The bottom of the barrel falls out, bits of burning wood are scattered far and wide, rivulets of flaming tar run down the hillside, and a shouting, jostling crowd scrambles for pieces of faggot which will be kept for luck and protection throughout the year, or sent to Burghead men living overseas.

10

Twelfth-night and Christmas-end

THE Feast of the Epiphany marks the end of the Twelve Days of Christmas, though not of the ecclesiastical Christmas season. Strictly speaking, the Twelve Days end on Epiphany Eve, but since the following day is a high festival of the Church and was formerly a holiday, it is usually regarded as the last of Christmas as well as an important celebration in its own right. For this reason it is often called Twelfth-day (or Twelfth-night in northern countries where time

was anciently reckoned by nights) and sometimes, more correctly, Thirteenth-day.

In England it is also called Old Christmas Day,
because it coincides with the date of Christmas in
the unreformed calendar used before 1752. In
that year the British Isles were brought into line
with other countries by the adoption of the
Gregorian calendar. To achieve this, eleven days
had to be arbitrarily eliminated, so that Septem-
ber 2, 1752, was immediately followed by Sep-
tember 14. This meant that all subsequent festivals came eleven days earlier, which caused a
good deal of confusion and some alarm in simple
minds. Many people clung to the Old Style dates
and continued to celebrate Christmas and numerous other anniversaries eleven, twelve or thirteen
days after their New Style counterparts. In time,
of course, this particular manifestation of conserv-
atism died out, but here and there we see traces of
it in customs that rightly belong to one day in the
month and are observed on another, and in the
still-remembered names of Old Christmas Day,
Old New Year, Old May Day, and many more.

Epiphany is the feast of the Manifestation of
Christ to the Gentiles, and the special festival of
the Three Kings who represented the world beyond Jewry on that far-off day. In churches where
Christmas Cribs are displayed, the figures of the
shepherds are removed then and those of the

Wise Men substituted, and the same is done in private houses where model Cribs are erected. In some homes the long journey to Bethlehem is re-enacted by placing the Kings in a remote corner of the room on Christmas Eve and gradually bringing them a little nearer every day until finally the Crib is reached on January 6. In London gifts of gold, frankincense and myrrh are offered on behalf of the Queen in the Chapel Royal. Formerly the presentation was made by the sovereign in person, but when George III's madness made this temporarily impossible, a proxy had to be appointed, and this has been the custom ever since. Similar royal gifts were once made in Spain, where, as we have seen, the Three Kings are themselves the gift-bringers for all children.

In southern Germany and Austria boys go about in bands of four during the Octave of Epiphany, singing carols known as star songs. The leader carries a gold star upon a pole, and the other three are dressed as the Kings, one having a soot-blackened face to represent Balthazar of Saba. In some districts they carry a Crib about with them, and if any house is found to be without one of its own, they leave it there. Elsewhere in Europe, children in masks run about shouting and knocking on doors, or long and noisy torchlit processions wind through the streets with bells clanging, horns blowing and whips cracking.

These are purification rites, intended to drive away ghosts and evil spirits, and probably, like Befana in Italy and the strange skin-clad Berchtel who capers and prances on Epiphany Eve in Carinthia, they really belong to the pagan spring festival, and are much older than the Christian feast with which they are now connected.

In Gloucestershire formerly farmhands went into the fields early on the morning of January 6, and lit thirteen fires there, a large one for Our Lord and twelve smaller ones for the Twelve Apostles. As soon as Judas' fire was kindled, it was stamped out. The others were left to burn away, to bring luck to the crops, and afterward the men were given plum cake or seedcake and cider. In Herefordshire the wassail bowl was carried into the cow byre, where toasts were drunk to the cattle, and a cake with a hole in the center was placed on the horn of an ox. If he tossed it off, it was a sign of good luck, and according to whether it fell before or behind the animal, the bailiff or the farmer's wife had the right to claim it.

These customs have died out now, but there is one form of wassailing that still survives in a few cider-apple districts. On Twelfth-night, or in some places Old Twelfth-night (January 17), bands of men go to the orchards at dusk with lanterns and shotguns, and fire through the branches of the trees. Cider is poured around the roots, and toast or cake soaked in cider is set in the fork. This is done for luck now, or perhaps simply because it is an old and pleasant custom, but there is no doubt that it was once a seriously performed magical rite, intended to make the trees bear plentifully in the coming season. Indeed, the traditional song that is sung during the proceedings makes this quite clear, for in it the trees are addressed as living, thinking beings, their good health invoked, and their utmost efforts requested to:

> ". . . bear apples enow,
> Hats full, Caps full,
> Three score bushels full,
> And my pockets full too."

In Greece, and every other country that belongs to the Eastern Church, a ceremony known as the Blessing of the Waters takes place at Epiphany in honor of Our Lord's Baptism. Sometimes it is the sea that is blessed, sometimes a river or pool, or it may be simply water brought into the church for the purpose. Along the coast a procession of clergy and people goes down to the shore, and there the bishop throws a cross into the water, withdraws it by means of a long ribbon, and sprinkles the assembled people with the drops that cling to it. In some places what is perhaps an older form of the rite is used. Here the cross is not withdrawn by the bishop but is left in the water, and young men dive in and struggle to retrieve it. He who succeeds in doing so is treated with honor, and enjoys various privileges for the rest of the day.

This custom has been observed for many years now at Tarpon Springs, Florida, where many of the sponge fishers are of Greek descent. On January 6, locally known as Greek Cross Day, a colorful procession goes at noon, through streets gay with bunting, from St. Nicholas' Church down to Spring Bayou. There passages from Scripture are read in Greek and in English, and a white dove is released as a symbol of the Holy Spirit. Then the archbishop flings a small gold cross into the water, and twenty or thirty young divers plunge in after it. The man who finds it restores it to the archbishop, and receives a special blessing from him. Since 1952 this ceremony has also been held at Long Beach, California.

Cakes have always been associated with the Twelfth-night feast. Until well into the nineteenth century, every French, Dutch, German and English family had its Twelfth-cake, often a very splendid confection, dark with fruit and spices, heavily iced, and decorated with gold and silver stars, many-colored flowers, crowns, dragons and little figures of the Three Kings. Each cake contained a bean and a pea; the man who found the bean in his portion was the Twelfth-night King, and the girl who found the pea was the Queen. If the bean was found by a girl, she had the right to choose her own king and, similarly, a man finding the pea chose the queen. In some parts of France, when the cake was cut, two portions were set aside for God and Our Lady. These were never eaten by any in the company, but were given to the first poor person who came to the house. The rest, carefully divided into exactly as many parts as there were people at the feast, was distributed by the youngest boy present.

Twelfth-cakes are rarely seen now in ordinary households, but at Drury Lane Theatre the Baddeley Cake is annually cut after the performance on January 6. This is done in memory of Robert Baddeley, who was a chef in his younger days and afterwards became an actor. When he died in 1794 he left £100 to pay for wine and a cake, to be shared on Twelfth-night by the company then playing at Drury Lane. So year by year a large iced cake is carried into the Green Room by the theater attendants in their eighteenth-century livery and powdered wigs, and there it is cut in the presence of the assembled players, who afterward drink to the memory of the actor-chef.

At Haxey in Lincolnshire a very ancient game known as the Hood Game is played on January 6. Tradition says it began in the thirteenth century, and a pleasant little story is told to explain how this happened. Almost certainly, however, it is older than the modern players claim, and some folklorists believe it had its origin in pagan spring rites. There are twelve official players known as "Boggans," who by tradition must always have something red in their dress. Their leader is the King Boggan, and they are accompanied by a Fool, who opens the proceedings by mounting a stone near the church and making a traditional speech. Then follows the ceremony of smoking the Fool. A fire of dampened straw is lit below the stone, and clouds of smoke pour out around the man standing above. In 1956 someone forgot to dampen the straw and the Fool's clothes caught fire, but the flames were soon beaten out, and no one minded. When the speechmaking and smoking are ended, all go to a piece of high ground called the Hoodlands, and the real game begins.

The Boggans stand in a wide ring, with the King Boggan and a crowd of men from Haxey and Westwoodside in the center. The King Boggan throws up the first "hood," a tightly rolled piece of canvas securely tied, and everyone scrambles to seize and carry it past the waiting ring of Boggans to his own village. If this can be done, that hood is "dead," but if not, it has to be returned to the King and played again.

Several canvas hoods are thus thrown, and when all have been disposed of, the Sway is brought into

action. This is the last hood, made of a length
of very stout rope encased in leather. As soon as
it is thrown, the circle is broken, eager hands are
laid on the hood, and the whole company surges
off the Hoodlands, as every man present tries to
get the Sway to one or other of the three inns in
the parish. A solid mass of men, like a vast Rugby
scrum, slowly pushes and heaves its way down to
the village, sweeping aside every obstacle in its
path, including hedges and walls. Victory is
achieved when the supporters of a particular inn
finally manage to get the Sway through its doors.
Then there are free drinks for all and much lively
rejoicing, and the rest of the day is spent in merrymaking of various kinds. The Sway remains in the
winning inn until Haxey Day comes round again.

For most people Twelfth-night means the end
of Christmas, when holly and ivy are taken down,
and French children go about singing a little carol
of farewell that begins:

"Noël is leaving us, sad it is to tell,
But he will come again.
Adieu, Noël."

In fact, it is not quite the end, for the ecclesiastical festival extends to Candlemas Day, when
candles are blessed in many churches, and old-
fashioned people prophesy from the day's weather
the late or early arrival of spring. In Jedburgh
it is called Candlemas Ba' Day, because a riotous

game of handball is played in the streets then between the Uppies and the Downies, or men from
above and below the Mercat Cross. Between
Twelfth-night and Candlemas there are still a few
anniversaries to be observed, like Plow Monday
in England, with its plow-blessings and its north-
country sword dances and Mumming plays; St.
Knut's Day (January 13) in Sweden, which is
Yule-end there; and at Lerwick in the Shetland
Isles the splendid fire-festival of Up Helly-aa, or
Twenty-fourth Night, which is held in the latter
half of January.

The Shetlands were Scandinavian islands until
1469 and the people of Lerwick remember this
at Up Helly-aa. A Norse war galley, dragon-
headed, with shields overside, and large enough to
hold twelve mail-coated, wing-helmeted guisers,
is dragged through the streets on a wheeled chassis,
accompanied by other guisers in Viking dress, two
bands playing Norse, Scottish and English airs,
and three or four hundred torchbearers. The procession goes slowly down from the town center
to the shore, and there the torchbearers make a
wide circle, the crew disembark, and their captain,
the Guiser Jarl, calls upon all to join in singing
"The Norseman's Home." When the song is
ended, there is a moment's silence; then a bugle is
blown, and at once all the burning torches are
flung into the empty galley. The flames leap high

in the air as the ship catches fire, maroons sound from Fort Charlotte and sirens from ships in the harbor, fireworks are let off, and the noise of cheering and shouting goes on till the galley is burned to ashes. Afterwards the guisers go round to all the inns and cafés, and are entertained as luck-bringers, and in many places there is feasting and dancing until well into next morning.

In earlier times the celebrations were simpler, though just as noisy. Blazing tar barrels used to be pushed around the streets, and it was not until 1855 that these were replaced by the more orderly torchlight procession. The Norse galley is an even newer feature and dates from 1894. But though its details have changed, the Up Helly-aa festival is very old, and by its fires, masquerades, music and feasting, Yule-end has been celebrated in Shetland from time immemorial.

11

Christmas Legends and Superstitions

LEGENDS and superstitions of many kinds surround the Christmas season, some purely Christian in origin, and some rooted in ancient pagan traditions of the Winter Solstice. Many are concerned with animals, birds or plants. In earlier times no one doubted that every living creature shared in the wonder of the Nativity, or that, just as each one in his manner had worshiped the newborn Child on the first Christmas Day, so his descendants continued to do on every succeeding anniversary.

The raven is said to have been the first bird to

know what had happened, for he was flying over the Bethlehem fields when the sky was suddenly filled with angels; but the cock was the first to proclaim the event, crying *Christus natus est,* and ever since then cocks have crowed all through the night of December 24. In Normandy the wren is called *Poulette de Dieu,* because she brought moss and feathers to make a coverlet for the Christ Child in the manger. The cow, too, did her best to warm Him with her breath, and since then her breath has been sweeter than that of any other animal. A very widespread tradition says that as midnight strikes on Christmas Eve, the cattle turn to the east and kneel down in the byre, the horses kneel in the stable and blow upon the manger, and the bees hum the Hundredth Psalm in their hives. In some European lands all animals are believed to have the power of speech then; but it is dangerous for human beings to listen to their talk, and many stories are told of dire misfortunes that befell people who were unwise enough to do so.

Trees are often thought to break into blossom, or bend their branches downward in reverence on holy night. In France the Christmas rose is said to have sprung up when the angel Gabriel touched the ground with his staff, so that a little girl who accompanied the shepherds might have flowers to offer the Holy Child. Another tale says every shepherd brought some little gift. One gave a lambskin, another a whistle, a third his own favorite tabor, and a fourth a rattle. One, however, had nothing except a daisy which he had picked on the way. The Child touched it with His lips, whereupon the petals turned red along the edges, and since that night many daisies have had rose-tipped petals.

In England the Holy Thorn blooms on Old Christmas Eve. Legend relates that when St. Joseph of Arimathea came to Britain to preach the Gospel, he journeyed to Glastonbury and there, on Wearyall Hill, he thrust his thornwood staff into the ground. It took root and grew, and every year it blossomed at midnight on Christmas Eve. When the calendar was changed in 1752, many watched to see whether it would flower on the old date or the new, and the fact that it did so on the former confirmed numerous people in their belief that this, and not the day ordained by Parliament, was the true anniversary.

The old Glastonbury Thorn was wantonly destroyed during the Puritan period, but by then cuttings had been taken from it and planted elsewhere. Thus it has several descendants, including one in the ruins of Glastonbury Abbey itself. These daughter trees bloomed in the same manner, and some, especially one at Orcop in Herefordshire, are still visited by many people on the night of January 5, in the hope of seeing the buds break at the traditional hour. Not infrequently they do so, for these hawthorns belong to a winter-flowering variety which blossoms twice in the year, once at or near Epiphanytide, and then again in the spring. At Orcop the opening of the buds at about midnight on Old Christmas Eve has been recorded several times.

Telling ghost stories around the fire is a favorite Christmas pastime; but concerning the ghosts themselves, there are two distinct traditions. One is that on this holy night no spirit wanders abroad, and no witch or evil creature has power to harm. Shakespeare mentions this belief, which is still held by many. Elsewhere, however, the tradition is otherwise. Formerly, in Scandinavia trolls were said to hold high revel in the Christmas season, and the dead also returned to their homes, as in Roman Catholic countries they did at All Souls. When the Christmas Eve festivities were ended, the living retired to rest, leaving a bright fire burning, candles lit, and the table spread with food and drink. Any unusual sounds heard during the hours of darkness were carefully ignored, for it was the dead moving about below who made them. In Brittany similar preparations were made in case the Virgin Mary should pass that way, and in the Tyrol milk was left for her and for the Christ Child.

In northern Europe the Wild Hunt could sometimes be heard riding past with shouts and the bay-
ing of hounds. This was a cavalcade of spectral
horsemen, who were thought in some countries to
be the old gods come again, and in others to be demons, or the souls of the evil dead, or of unbap-
tized children. Their leader might be Odin, or the
Devil, or some famous hero like King Arthur or
Hugh Capet, or he might be some local master of
hounds condemned to lead the rout for ever
because he had hunted on Sunday. But whoever
the riders were, and whoever led them, they were
dangerous to mortals, and must never under any
circumstances be looked at as they rushed furiously
by.

Many ancient beliefs, some quite vanished now
and some still living, cling round particular days
in the season. Greenery for decorations should not
be brought in until Christmas Eve, and at Candlemas it must be taken down without fail, or bad
luck will follow. Few people run this latter risk,
for normally rooms are cleared on the day after
Twelfth-night, but formerly it was not uncommon
for house decorations to remain until the very end
of the season. It was when they were accidentally
left for one day too long that danger threatened.
Bread and cakes baked on Christmas morning,
like those baked on Good Friday, were thought
to have special virtues. They never went mouldy

and, if kept until they were quite dry, and then powdered in hot water when the occasion arose, they could be (and still are in some country districts) used as a remedy for summer sickness and other ills.

If the first rays of the rising sun strike through apple trees on Christmas morning, a good crop may be expected. If anyone finds a ring or a coin in his or her portion of Christmas pudding, that is lucky, for the first means marriage within twelve months and the second wealth; but for a girl to find a thimble means continued spinsterhood. Children born on Christmas Eve or Day will be fortunate throughout life, and have the power to see spirits; and in Ireland it is said that those who die at midnight on Christmas Eve are fortunate too, for the gates of heaven stand wide open then, and the soul can pass straight through them without having to expiate his sins in purgatory.

The ominous associations of Holy Innocents' Day, or Childermas, are not often remembered now, but at one time this anniversary of child-murder and women's despair was considered so unlucky that even the day of the week on which it fell was tainted for the next twelve months. On such weekdays, as on the festival itself, nothing important was ever attempted, nor any new work begun. Household tasks were reduced to a minimum, little business was done, and even new clothes were not put on. It was useless to begin anything fresh then, for either it would never be finished, or it would have an unlucky ending.

New Year's Day was naturally important, not only in itself, but as a portent of the coming year, and even in this supposedly nonsuperstitious age it still is so for many. As late as the end of last century, it was considered very unlucky in Scotland and northern England to give fire out of the house for any purpose whatsoever, and if anyone sought a light for his pipe, or a brand to rekindle a fire accidentally gone out, he or she was almost certain to be refused. It was thought unwise to wash linen or sweep rooms on January 1, for thus the luck of the house would be washed or swept away; and though in many areas New Year's gifts were exchanged, nothing else was willingly given, lent or paid out, lest paying and giving should predominate over receiving in the coming year, and poverty result.

The weather of the Twelve Days is still carefully observed, both by the weatherwise and by the superstitious. "A green Christmas maketh a full churchyard" is an old saying which has a substratum of truth, since mild weather in December is often followed by a bitter January, especially trying for the old and the delicate. In Brittany it is said that the winds which prevail during the Twelve Days will blow throughout the year, that of the first day blowing in January, that of the second in February, and so on. In England the New Year's Eve winds foretell a good season if they blow from south or west, a good fruit year if from the east, and storms and disaster if from the north or northeast. The actual day of the week is to be noticed also, for tradition has it that a Monday Christmas portends a long, cold winter, with winds and storms; but a Wednesday Christmas or a Saturday New Year promises a fine summer, good harvests and plenty.

So we come at last to Candlemas Day and the final end of the Christmas season. This is the Feast of the Purification of Our Lady and the Presentation of the Child Jesus in the Temple. It owes its more familiar name to the custom, once universally observed and still kept up today in many parishes, of blessing candles in church and carrying them in procession, in honor of Christ Who came as "a light to lighten the Gentiles." At Blidworth in Nottinghamshire, the Presentation is remembered by a very charming ceremony known as Cradle Rocking. A cradle decorated with flowers and leaves is placed near the altar, and in it the baby last baptized in the parish is laid and gently rocked by the vicar for a few moments.

Candlemas has other traditions besides those connected with the ecclesiastical feast. It is the first clear milestone along the road to spring. By now the days are definitely lengthening, and the first snowdrops, sometimes called purification flowers, or Candlemas bells, have appeared. However bad the weather may be, there is a new and hopeful feeling in the air; and, indeed, this is one of the few days in the year when bad weather is welcomed, for a cold, hard Candlemas is said by countryfolk to be a sign of an early spring. Christmas, which first broke into light with the little flames on the Advent wreaths, burns to its lovely end in the glowing candle services, and now, as the natural and the ecclesiastical year swing around together, we begin to look toward spring and Easter. And so, as Herrick sang three hundred years ago,

"Down with the Rosemary and Bayes,
Down with the Mistleto;
Instead of Holly, now up-raise
The greener Box for show.
The Holly hitherto did sway;
Let Box now domineere,
Until the dancing Easter Day,
Or Easter's Eve appeare."

Books about Christmas

A Short Bibliography

Barnett, James H. *American Christmas*
New York: Macmillan Co., 1954

Campbell, R. J. *Story of Christmas*
New York: Macmillan Co., 1935

Count, Earl W. *Four Thousand Years of Christmas*
New York: Henry Schuman, 1953

Dearmer, P., ed. *Oxford Book of Carols*
London: Oxford University Press, 1928

Hole, Christina. *English Custom & Usage*
London: Batsford, Ltd., 1942

Krythe, Maymie R. *All About Christmas*
New York: Harper & Brothers, 1954

Meyer, Robert, Jr. *Festivals U.S.A.*
New York: Ives Washburn, Inc., 1950

Miles, C. A. *Christmas in Ritual and Tradition*
London: Unwin, 1912

Index

Advent, 14-18, 47
Advent wreaths, 14, 91
Alabama, 13
Alsace, 49
America, North, 13, 24, 26, 27, 31, 33, 34, 41, 43, 45, 48, 77
Angel Gabriel, 47, 84
Angus, Scotland, 69
Animal disguises, 12, 46, 47
Animals, 17, 38, 55, 56, 83, 84
Ashen Faggot, 31
Australia, 51, 63, 64
Austria, 45, 74, 86

Baddeley Cake, 78
Barring out schoolmaster, 17
Bees humming, 84
Befana, 48, 49, 75
Bells, 19, 62, 63, 65, 66
Belsnickel, 48
Berchtel, 75
Biggar, Lanarks, 69
Birds, 55, 83, 84
Birth at Christmas, 88
Blessing the plow, 19, 20, 81
   the water, 76, 77
Blidworth, Notts, 90
Boar's head ceremony, 52
Bonfires, 10, 32, 33, 49, 69, 75
Boxing Day, 37-39
Boy Bishop, 15, 16
Brittany, 86, 89
Burning the Clavie, 70, 71
Buttenmandln, 47

Cakes, 18, 70, 75-78, 87, 88
Calendar reform, 73, 85
California, 27, 77
Cambridge, 63
Candlemas, 14, 19, 30, 31, 80, 81, 87, 90, 91
Candlemas Ba' Day, 80, 81
Carinthia, 75

Carols at Christmas, 43, 52, 58-64
   at Easter, 60
   at Epiphany, 80
   at New Year, 69
Chapel Royal ceremony, 74
Childermas, See Holy Innocents
Christ Child, the, 7, 8, 29, 33, 37, 49, 50, 83-86
Christmas boxes, 37, 38, 62
   bull, 12
   candle, 29, 30
   cards, 39-41
   crib, 18, 27, 29, 73, 74
   date of, 8-10
   Day, Old, 73
   during Commonwealth, 12, 13, 43, 44, 59, 60
   Eve, Old, 85, 86
   "piece," 39
   pudding, 32, 53, 88
   trees, 19, 24-28, 37, 44, 62, 63
Colorado, 31
Crackers, 56
Cradle rocking, 90
Crowing of the Cock, 34

Dead returning at Christmas, 86
Death at Christmas, 88
Decorations, 10, 11, 19, 21-28, 30, 41, 80, 87
   taking down, 19, 80, 87
Demons, 17, 42, 46, 47, 50, 75, 86, 87
Denmark, 30, 54
Devil, the, 62, 87
Devonshire, 31
Dewsbury, Yorks, 62
Dies Natalis Invicti Solis, 9

Easter, 60, 91
Edinburgh, 69
Epiphany, 9, 14, 18, 19, 28, 37, 48, 72-81, 86

93

Epiphany—*cont.*
    gifts at, 37, 48, 74
European customs, 14-17, 22, 24,
    30, 32-34, 36-38, 43-50, 54, 55,
    68, 74-78, 80, 81, 86, 87
Evergreens, 10, 11, 18, 19, 21-28,
    30, 35, 67, 69, 87

Father Christmas, 15, 42-44, 49
Fire not given out at New Year,
    89
Fireball procession, 69
Firecrackers, 32
First-foot, 35, 66-68
Florida, 77
Flowers, 41, 84-86, 91
Food at Christmas, 17, 51-56, 87,
    88
France, 30, 37, 49, 59, 74, 78, 80,
    84, 86, 89
Furry dancers, 68

Games, 11, 32, 56, 70, 78-81
Germany, 14, 24, 25, 32, 45, 47-
    50, 55, 59, 74, 77
Ghosts, 46, 86
Glastonbury Thorn, 84, 85
Gloucestershire, 75
Good Friday, 87
Greece, 76, 77
Greek Cross Day, 77
Guise dancers, 12, 68, 81, 82
Gun firing, 32, 69, 70, 75, 76

Hallowe'en, 56
Hand-bell-ringing, 61
Handsel Monday, 37
Haxey Hood Game, 79, 80
Helston, Cornwall, 68
Herefordshire, 75, 85, 86
Hodening Horse, 12
Hogmanay, 69, 70
Holland, 15, 37, 45, 46, 77
Holy Innocents' Day, 15, 88, 89
Hungary, 55

Ireland, 30, 88
Italy, 37, 48, 49, 59, 75

Jedburgh, Roxburghshire, 80
Julklapp, 50
Julotte, 34

Kalends of January, 10-12, 21, 35,
    36

Kissing bough, 25, 26
Kissing under mistletoe, 23, 24
Knight Rupprecht, 42, 47, 48

Lerwick, Shetland, 81, 82
London, 27, 28, 63, 66, 74, 78
Lord of Misrule, 11, 13, 56
Lucia Queen, 16, 17, 49
Luther, Martin, 24

Macedonia, 68
Magi, The, *See* Three Kings
Manchester, 25, 66
Mari Lwyd. 12
Melbourne, Australia, 63, 64
Midnight Mass, 18, 32
Mistletoe, 18, 22-24, 91
Mock king, 11
Moravian vigil, 34
Mumming plays, 20, 39, 43, 81

Nativity, Feast of the, 8-10, 36
New Mexico, 33
New water, 68
New Year, 10-12, 30, 33-37, 55, 56,
    65-71, 89, 90
    gifts at, 11, 12, 35-37, 66-68,
        89
    Old, 70, 73
New York, 27
Nikolo-Weibl, 47
Nine Lessons service, 63
Normandy, 84
Norway, 30, 34

Odin, 44, 48, 50, 87
Orcop, Herefordshire, 85, 86
Oxford, 52, 54

Pagan festivals, 7, 9-12, 21, 35, 36,
    75
Pantomimes, 19, 39
Pennsylvania, 25, 34, 48
Plow Monday, 19, 20, 81
Plygain, 34
Poland, 54, 55, 68
Provence, 30
Purification, Feast of the, 90
Puritan dislike of Christmas, 12,
    13, 43, 44, 59

Roman winter festivals, 9-12, 21,
    35, 36
Royal broadcast at Christmas, 56,
    57

St. Boniface, 24
St. Francis of Assisi, 56, 59
St. Ives, Cornwall, 68
St. Joseph of Arimathea, 85
St. Knut's Day, 81
St. Lucia's Day, 16, 17, 37
St. Nicholas, 15, 37, 42-48
St. Peter, 47
St. Stephen's Day, 38
St. Thomas' Day, 17, 18
Santa Claus, See St. Nicholas
Saturnalia, 10, 11, 35
Scandinavia, 16, 22, 27, 30, 34, 37, 38, 50, 52, 54, 55, 86
Shetland Isles, 54, 81
Shrove Tuesday, 17
Silesia, 55
Somerset, 31, 32
Spain, 37, 46, 48, 59, 74
Star songs, 74
Stonehaven, Kincardine, 69
Stow, John, 22, 26
Strasbourg, 24
Sweden, 16, 37, 38, 50, 55, 60, 81
Switzerland, 45, 46
Sword dances, 19, 81
Syrian customs, 32, 33

Thirteenth-day, 73

Three Kings, The, 36, 42, 48, 73, 74, 77
Touch of Peace, 33
Twelth-night and Twelfth-day, 18, 19, 30, 32, 72-81, 87
     Old, 75
Twelve Days of Christmas, 14, 18, 19, 26, 30, 53, 54, 89
Twenty-fourth Night, 81

Up Helly-aa, 81, 82

Waits, 61, 62
Wales, 12, 33, 68
Wassail bowls, 54
Wassailing apple trees, 75, 76
Watch Night service, 65, 66
Weather beliefs, 80, 89-91
Westphalia, 49
Whistler, Lawrence, 41
Wick, Caithness, 69
Wigilia, 54
Wild Hunt, 87
Winter Solstice, 7, 10, 16, 17, 21, 44, 83

York, 23
Yule, 50, 52, 54, 81, 82
Yule Log, 31